CONTENTS

ORIGINAL ILLUSTRATIONS BY GAIL KA'UHANE. Photos courtesy of Archives of Hawaii. Front cover: Painting by Linda Varez, artist, from National Park Service Art Collection, Hawaii Volcanoes National Park.

Have you ever felt a tingle along your spine as you drove along the Pali on a moonless night?

If you have, check your car! Perhaps you are carrying pork in some form.

Whistling in the dark is one thing, but whistling in the house is something else entirely. Why?

Only ghosts whistle in the house!

When you visited Kilauea Crater, Madame Pele's volcanic home on the Big Island, did you eat the forbidden ohelo berries?

Unlucky you. Be prepared for misfortune—perhaps an accident!

Was that a shooting star you just saw? Or was it glowing phosphorescence? Or just a harmless firefly?

None of the above. It was Akualele, the dreaded flying god, bent on an errand of destruction!

Every ancient culture has its share of beliefs, superstitions, and fears, and the Hawaiians are no exception.

As a good friend and as a member of an Hawaiian family, I am grateful that my friends and relatives have seen fit to open their hearts to me and to trust me to relate the ancient beliefs and the stories that go with such beliefs.

How the reader chooses to interpret these stories is a matter that only the reader can decide. How much to believe, is, again, up to the reader. I can only testify that Islanders, both native and transplanted, have much regard for the ancient beliefs and customs. Such customs are a part of Hawaii's cultural heritage, and are still widely practiced in many parts of the Hawaiian Islands.

Islanders respect them.

So should the visitor.

Under The Spell

Kahuna assisting at a birth.

Although the Hawaiians had no written language until the coming of the missionaries in 1820, they were highly skilled in many industries in their own culture.

Their "professionals," or those they relied on to guide them, were the kahunas.

To a great many people, the word "kahuna" strikes immediate fear. "Witch doctor" is the first thought.

Actually the true meaning is priest, minister, sorcerer or an expert in any profession.

"Keeper of the secret" or "heart lore" are two other definitions.

Kahunas were always of the ali'i class and included surgeons, obstetricians, herb specialists, architects, navigators, musicians, artists and historians. Their source of knowledge was a carefully guarded secret and passed on to very specially chosen and trained followers. Sometimes as a kahuna lay dying, his successor would carefully wipe his lips while chanting, thereby receiving the last of the secrets.

The Kahuna

The medical kahuna relied on his knowledge of herbs, diet, and massage. Many of his remedies are still used today and are very effective. For example, the use of the aloe plant is unexcelled

for the relief and healing of burns. The plan can be found in many Island home gardens.

"'Awa," an extract of a shrub, was used as a narcotic drink. Useful as a sedative for medical procedures such as setting broken bones, 'awa figured largely in ceremonies conducted by certain kahunas to exorcise troublesome spirits or to placate the gods.

Some Hawaiian medicines are being investigated today by medical men. In particular is an "anti-cancer" serum concocted from a certain sea worm. It has been tested on animals and has arrested certain types of carcinoma.

The medical kahunas were skilled in combining religion and psychology.

The most dreaded of the kahunas were the kahuna 'ana 'ana, who had the power to pray persons to death. Modern medical men admit that this is possible. A severe emotional and mental state brought on by the belief that he was being "prayed to death" would first of all induce a serious fall in a person's blood pressure. This, coupled with a lack of food and water could very easily bring on death.

In order to be effective magic, the victim of this sorcery must believe in the power of the sorcerer, and his intelligence must be a step lower than that of the kahuna.

To effectively perform his black art, the kahuna had to have some personal possession belonging to the victim. A lock of hair, nail parings or spittle were things carefully guarded, especially by those of the ali'i class who assigned special guardians to dispose of these things secretly.

Today in Hawaii there are stiff penalties under the law for practicing death sorcery or pretending to have that power.

Other types of kahunas are:

The Kahuna Aloha, the love inducing specialist.

Kahuna Pule, preacher, pastor, priest, prayer expert.

Kahuna Ho'opi 'opi 'o, one who inflicts illness by gesture such as rubbing his own head to inflict a severe headache on his victim.

Kahuna Lomilomi, a masseur.

Kahuna Ho'ohanau, obstetrician—

It is doubtful if the kahuna was a fan of women's liberation, but all the same he had the power to grant the expectant mother a painless experience. To do this, he would take the travail upon himself. And because birth was a "family affair," he also was able to transfer the pain upon the father.

The power and influence of the kahuna as a figure of religious authority is still very much alive today, although in some instances their feats are not discussed openly or freely by Islanders. However, modern kahunas (priests or ministers) figure very actively in dedications and blessings of new buildings, roads, bridges, hotels, and even homes.

Even after the missionaries introduced Christianity to the Islands, many of the old customs were still adhered to and practiced by the Hawaiians, especially when it came to birth, marriage and death.

Some of the notions and customs relating to birth were as follows:

When an expectant mother wished to know if her child would be a boy or a girl, she consulted a kahuna pale

Unusual Customs Then And Now

keiki, who would say, "Show me your hand." If she put out the right hand, the baby would be a boy, and if the left, a girl.

A pregnant woman was not supposed to wear a lei because this would cause the umbilical cord to strangle the child.

A kahuna could allow the mother to have a painless birth experience by passing on the pain to another person or an animal, even the father himself.

The crushed leaves of a beach morning glory, rubbed on the opu (stomach) was an aid to childbirth.

The placenta (iewe) was washed and buried under a tree. Failure to wash it caused the baby to have weak eyes.

The story is told that in the district of Puna, it was the custom to put the washed placenta on the highest branch of a hala tree, where it would be safe from the rats. The children of this district were born with long eyelashes that stood out like the prickles on the hala leaf. People from other areas teased these people calling them "maka kokala" (prickle eyes).

At the moment of birth, if the child turned his face toward his mother, he would always love her best, if toward the midwife or father, he would love them best.

If a child was born face down he would always excel at chanting, even if he happened to have a poor voice.

There was a case of a baby born without ears and the family was ter-

ribly distressed so they took the child to a kahuna lapaau. He felt the child's head over very carefully and then with a smile informed the parents that the little ears were actually there, curled up like tiny rosebuds under the skin. Later, they took the baby to a hospital, and slits were made and the tiny ears were released.

The piko (navel) was very important. The word was used to mean "closely related." An often used greeting among Hawaiians was "Pehea ko piko?" (How is your navel?) This phrase is not used commonly today as it can be misunderstood.

The Hawaiian people admired and revered the human body. Many babies at birth, especially those of the ali'i class, were massaged and molded with experienced hands in order to insure the child growing up beautifully formed. The parents carefully massaged them daily until in time they developed normally.

Babies' heads were massaged (lomilomi) and molded from the moment of birth; they were not allowed to sleep on their faces and were constantly turned.

It was customary to give the first born son to the father's parents and a first born daughter to the mother's parents. This custom, and the fact that in the early days children's births were

Tatooing, a widespread practice in Hawaii, was more than mere decoration. It also served to identify the aumakua or family of gods to which the tatooed person belonged.

not recorded, made it extremely difficult to trace a person's genealogy. To add to this confusion, children's names were often changed.

Children were seldom whipped in the old days but were pounded on the knee.

The head was considered sacred as it was the crown of the body. To strike a child or anyone on the head was an insult.

If a kahuna was called upon to exorcise an evil spirit from a person's body, his procedure was to pull the spirit out from under the big toenail. It was necessary that the evil spirit be kept as far away from the head of the bewitched body, and what was farther than the toenail?

If an infant wet the clothing or bedding of an unrelated person, that person could claim the baby as his own. Members of royalty have been known to deliberately place a coveted baby on a bed belonging to them, claiming it for their own when it wet the bedding. Parents with a surplus of children sometimes welcomed and tried to arrange such a situation. Not only would it be one less mouth to feed but it would mean great honor for the child and the family.

On a darker note—royalty also had the right to kill the child.

MARRIAGE:

Among royalty, a marriage between brother and sister was not considered incestuous but was for the purpose of keeping the blood line pure and so the mana (divine power believed to be possessed by royalty) would not be diluted.

Marriage between commoners needed no celebration. It was considered "just a pebble to pelt the rat."

When a boy began to show sexual awareness or interest, he was allowed to experiment for himself. If he were of the ali'i class, he was implicitly instructed by an older chiefess.

One of the most beautiful and useful customs of the Hawaiians is the ho'oponopono which is defined as "to set right, to restore and keep good relationship among family members." This was done by calling a meeting of all members of the family together, including anyone outside the family who might be involved or interested.

A healing kahuna or a senior member of the family would be in charge.

The gathering would begin and end with prayers to the gods or God. Confessions were made, discussion was lengthy, truthfulness and complete honesty were stressed. Causes of sickness were unearthed by this method. Misunderstandings and grievances were settled and restitution made when necessary.

In ancient days, the ho'oponopono was concluded by pani (closing rituals) which consisted of animal offerings to the gods. In modern times, a simple meal would suffice.

DEATH, BURIAL, AND FUNERAL CUSTOMS:

Until the moment of burial, the spirit of the departed was believed to be very close to the corpse. The mourners talked to it, scolded it or just reminisced.

Before the introduction of Christianity and Western influence, the custom of removing flesh from the bones and preserving and hiding the bones was the accepted method. Today, the funeral and burial, as we know them, are accepted.

Placing objects, dear or significant to the departed, in the coffin may still be done—a Bible, a piece of jewelry, special clothing, or a child's stuffed animal. Food, a lantern, or a canned beverage is often placed in the grave itself, the theory being that the spirit is still nearby.

Sometimes the family and friends of the deceased would take an entirely different route home after the burial, to confuse the spirit and prevent it from following.

Aumakua, the spiritual ancestors, were very real to the Hawaiians. When a person died, his spirit could take one of many forms—an owl, a bird, an eel or shark, a lizard or a rock. One could pray through his aumakua to the gods. The aumakua acted as an intermediary. It warned of approaching danger or misfortune, gave advice, and

had even been known to play tricks when in a mischievous mood.

Signs of grief following the loss of a loved one or particularly a member of the ali'i class took many forms in ancient times. Wailing was especially important and there were those who specialized in it. Knocking out teeth, disfiguring the face and body, suicide in order to join the deceased were practices customary in pre-missionary days but are seldom heard of today.

If a person who was ill or unconscious had to be carried out of the house for any reason, he must not be carried head first, as that was the method used for removing a corpse.

Never leave an open hole anywhere whether it has been made by man or animal. An open hole signifies a grave.

If you have been cursed, reverse it immediately and it will return to its sender.

Bodily afflictions were the result of a sin or fault. For example, the story is told of a woman who was a notorious gossip, causing great harm and grief to others. She had a stroke one day and was speechless until the day of her death. Her husband claimed this was just punishment.

A person who was a thief would develop trouble with one or both of his hands, perhaps a rash or pain or weakness.

Trouble with the feet indicated that a person was going in the wrong places.

Pity the poor man who suffered pain in the groin; he had been unfaithful!

Mana is a word of many meanings but it is best known to indicate supernatural or divine power or authority. The ali'i or the kahunas possessed this ability in various degrees. Even a rock could have mana, therefore it should not be removed from its original place unless proper ceremonies are carried out. Many people who have even innocently removed or disturbed such a rock have told of disaster, "bad luck," or even death following, until the rock was returned.

9

There are still little customs that cling, here in modern Hawaii. Here are a few:

Do not sit on a kapa (the beautiful hand-made Hawaiian quilts). Some believe this is bad luck; others claim it is just a matter of respect for the endless hours of loving labor put into the needle work.

If you have been presented with a lei, do not take it off your neck and present it to another person except a member of the immediate family and then only with the permission of the donor. The custom of throwing a lei overboard from a ship, believing if it floats to shore, the departing one will surely return, is not a truly Hawaiian custom.

Hawaiians, ancient and modern, are known for their hospitality. A stranger was always offered food (and shelter if needed) regardless of how much or how little a person possessed. It was considered rude not to offer food, or to eat in the presence of one who was not eating.

This custom is still carried out and to refuse to partake of another's food is extremely rude. To the host, not eating may signify that the food is not good enough or is possibly poisoned.

The poi bowl was the center of the meal and once it was uncovered, no quarrelling or bickering was allowed.

To wear another's clothing, especially a garment worn close to the skin, was forbidden. The person's mana was on that garment.

Many years ago, the older people objected or refused to go to hospitals that insisted they wear the gowns provided. Gowns with slit backs were especially abhorred because to reveal the "back-side" to anyone was insulting.

Visitors to Hawaii are introduced to a greeting using the word "Aloha." In large groups or gatherings, conventions and also churches, the moderator will often shout out "A-lo-o-o-o-ha!" and the audience is supposed to answer the same, stretching out the word and with great volume and gusto. This is *not* an Hawaiian custom. It was reportedly introduced by an elevator operator in the old Surfrider Hotel in the 1940's.

The word "Aloha" is a beautiful word full of meaning not only of love, but also of appreciation, welcome and farewell, and is more often said softly, and sincerely, and with great warmth.

If the blossom of the ohia tree, a flamboyant, crimson flower named, "lehua," is picked, it will rain.

The green ti plant is the truly Hawaiian one. The red ti was introduced in recent years and is strictly ornamental, and is also used at funerals.

Buildings, bridges, boats and roads require a blessing ceremony before use to insure safety, luck and prosperity.

One often sees a sign reading "Cross at your own risk, this bridge has not been blessed."

Everyone is familiar with the road signs throughout the Islands, designating historical sites. They depict a little figure of King Kamehameha, complete with feather cape and head piece. Some years ago when the Hawaii Visitors Bureau first put up the markers, the King had his arm outstretched, pointing to the site. Some Hawaiian people objected, their reason being "royalty doesn't point." Since then, all the signs were changed.

A sleeping person should not be awakened. He must be allowed to wake up naturally because during sleep his spirit is wandering and may not have returned to his body.

Aumakua

The Hawaiians believed that the aumakua, their ancestors, lived in that awesome place called Po, or eternity; a sea of time, a place where sea, sky and land are one and where time is no more.

The ancestors were transfigured into gods or god-spirits, who possessed great power and yet remained relatives, full of love and concern for those of their earthly family. They gave strength and comfort when needed, warning when danger threatened. They also inspired particular crafts and feats. They judged actions and were capable of meting out punishment when they felt it was necessary.

"Po" is the Hawaiian word for eternity, realm of the gods, chaos, hell, night, darkness, obscurity. There are many "jumping off"places into the realm of "Po." One is near Kaena Point in the Waianae District, another at South Point on the Island of Hawaii.

There was an eternal reward for the living. "Please the gods during life and you will join the aumakua after death."

The great fear many people had was that the deceased had somehow displeased the gods and there was no assurance that he had joined the aumakua. Perhaps he was wandering, homeless and hungry, feeding on spiders, butterflies and moths.

A genuine "Hawaiian" miracle — or so goes the story.
On the day of an earthquake, a man's
wife, delicate and less than half his weight, is able to lift
an enormous beam of lumber from her
husband's legs by calling on her aumakua to help.

If one had lived a reasonably good life and tried to please the gods, he would take his turn at the moment of death, after entering Po and become the aumakua himself.

On the contrary, the greatest tragedy was not to be received by the aumakua after death, but to be doomed to an existence of wandering forever, homeless and hungry and welcomed nowhere, just a lapu (ghost). In fact, hunger was the Hawaiians' idea of hell.

The Hawaiians laid great stress on the family ('ohana) and the aumakua remained always as loving members of the family. They were approachable, unlike the akuas who were awesome and impersonal. The aumakua could intercede between man and the gods.

The aumakua also gave superhuman strength to mortals when it was needed. During a severe earthquake on the Island of Hawaii, a building collapsed, pinning a hefty two-hundred-and-fifty pound man under the debris. He was completely helpless and in great pain as an enormous beam of lumber lay across his legs. His wife, a tiny one-hundred pound woman, called on her aumakua for help and putting her frail arms under the beam, she was able to lift it, and move it to the side. Her husband recovered from his injuries and later, his wife tried to repeat the feat with the same beam and was completely unable to even raise it an inch. She and her family gave credit to their aumakua.

There was a ceremony whereby the dead could be sent to the family aumakua. It was called "kaku'ai." The flesh was removed from the body and the bones were wrapped in tapa. The remains or just a part of the body such as hair, fingernails, or bones, were taken to either the volcano or the sea, depending on whom the family was related to. An offering was made, generally a live pig and awa, which were thrown in with the corpse. Then, the prophet prayed to the particular god to accept this one into the family of aumakuas.

This "transfiguration" process made it clear to the living that the departed one was physically gone forever although his spirit continued to exist.

The aumakua had many duties. They could comfort, punish, advise, warn, or even possess.

They could be naughty or mischievous.

They could also be adventurous.

At the moment of death, not all spirits made the direct leap into Po. One of the reasons could be that the relatives refused to release the spirit by practicing "unihipili", clinging to the dead by keeping some personal possession such as the bones, or even blood, in the home and deifying them.

In other words, they could not emotionally separate themselves from the dead.

The souls of people who were not aumakuas or had not been accepted by them were doomed to wander as ghosts or lapu and were greatly feared.

The story teller in ancient times was a respected, admired, and much sought after individual. He was called, "Ha'i mo'olelo." He or she was extremely talented in holding his audiences spellbound, both by manner, gestures, tone of voice and facial expressions, as well as by the content of the story. The story teller was blessed with a remarkable memory, as is evidenced even today in the recital of chants, which are intricate and endless. After all, the Hawaiian language was not put into writing until the arrival of the first missionaries in 1820.

When a sacred tale was being recited, no one could move or pass in front of the narrator.

The following are short stories, gathered with great difficulty in some cases, as many local people are reluctant to recount their experiences to anyone except a tolerant, broad-minded person whom they feel will not ridicule them or consider them ignorant. Some will share their experiences with great reverence and seriousness while others will remark, "I just heard or overheard this tale as a child. My grandparents really believed it, but...!" (followed by a shrug of the shoulders.)

Most of the stories are heresay only, and probably have never been printed before, to the author's knowledge. They are also often contradictory.

Stories: Personal

...cats were unknown in ancient days...the first ones were probably brought over in foreign ships.

My great grandmother was terrified of the furry creatures, believing them to be from the devil. She would lock herself in the house until help came if she even saw a cat in her yard. No one could convince her of their harmlessness or their usefulness. Horrified, she had watched them catch and torment lizards, which were one of her aumakuas.

One night, following a heated argument with her neighbor over the ownership of a branch of lychee fruit overhanging their shared fence, the neighbor decided to take revenge. Knowing the fear the old woman had of cats, the

And Heresay

neighbor crawled through my great-grandmother's bedroom window, first making sure the old woman was snoring loudly. Quickly and gently, she poured the oil from a can of tuna generously over the woman's chest and blan-ket and pillow. Leaving as silently as she had entered, she awaited the results. It wasn't long before at least a half-dozen neighbor-hood cats, attracted by the pun-gent odor of the oil, were crawling through her window (there were no screen on the old houses).

The poor old lady awoke, feeling the sensation of being licked to death. When she opened her eyes and saw the cats, she was con-vinced she was being consumed by the demons of Hell. She died of a heart attack.

We learned the truth later, when the neighbor broke down and confessed under the persistent questioning of a kahuna pule.

...if on a moonless night, you see flickering lights coming your way ...run!

My husband and I were taking a night walk in a remote part of Ka'u. We especially were enjoying the skies and the myriads of stars which we seldom saw while living in the city. Suddenly we heard the lowing of cattle in the distance. My husband calmed my fears by explaining that the cows and calves on a nearby ranch had been separated that morning and they were bawling for each other. However, this was followed by voices and soft laughter. In the distance, with the blackness of the a'a lava as a background and with a moonless sky, we saw the flickering of lights moving slowly toward us. My husband grabbed my hand and we fled back to our ranch house, breaking all speed records. We had just witnessed the dreaded "night marchers," the army of the dead. Woe unto anyone crossing their path; nothing but disaster and death would follow unless they happened to be one's aumakua.

...there are divided opinions among Hawaiians as to how best to fight an evil spirit. "Never face the evil," say some. "Show no fear," say others. "If you do not believe in the power of the evil, it cannot hurt you!"

In a particular fire station, situated in one of the most frequented paths of the "night marchers" (alii ghosts who march at night) one fireman was awakened suddenly out of sound sleep. He felt as if he were being choked. He struggled repeatedly and tried to call for help. His fellow firemen were aroused and managed to calm him, but the terrified man was convinced he had been visited by a lapu (ghost). His terror was transmitted to some of the other firefighters. Those who believed as he did crowded together in a different room to escape the evil ghost. There, they spent a sleepless night together. Others, who did not believe in the ghost and refused to acknowledge that there was anything evil attacking the man slept blissfully on in their own beds.

16

...ti leaves, used by ancient and modern Islanders for cooking, decorations, and as a poultice for the relief of headaches, also figure prominently in another way...

As recently as six months ago, a woman descending in an elevator in a beautiful new condominium on Ala Moana Blvd. was attacked and beaten. The afternoon following the assault, a ti leaf was placed on the floor of each elevator, as protection in the future. To this date, there has been no further trouble.

...can ghosts ever be good neighbors? Not according to the Hawaiians.

Question: What do ghosts (lapu) do? What are their habits?

Answer: They trip up people in the dark.
Pinch and pull limbs in bed.
Choke the throat
Scare horses.
Knock on houses.
Sour fresh milk.
Frighten babies.
Crumble stone walls.
Emit uncanny odors.
Mutter and chirp.
Cause weight on chest.

In the dark, they show their presence by the peculiar aroma of some scented tapa that may have been placed over the body after death.

Some remedies to ward off evil: hedges of ti leaves, also live coals of fire.

...there are conflicting stories and opinions as to who the *menehunes* were. Some claim they are equivalent to fairies, elves or leprechauns. Others say they were a race of little people, perhaps pygmies who used to inhabit the Islands, helpful little people who built fish ponds and repaired stone walls but were never seen, working only at night. They were also considered to be inquisitive, curious and mischievous.

During the recent restoration of Iolani Palace, one of the upstairs bedrooms had been completed. The windows and doors were locked securely, an automatic alarm set and a guard posted.

In the morning when the Palace was re-opened, the transom in the door of the bedroom was found opened. Little footprints led from the door across the floor up on to the bed and out the window. Menehunes?

...bones were precious...some of them were lucky charms.

As late as 1882 robbers hid out in Makua Valley in order to seize and kill unwary and rare travelers through that lonely area. They especially sought and treasured hairless legs out of which fish hooks could be made from the bones. These were especially lucky for catching aku.

...there is a heiau at Pokai Bay in Waianae. During "Kane's Night," you can plainly hear chants, the music of stringed instruments, and the smell of Hawaiian tobacco.

I live on the Waianae Coast. There is a cove near Kaena Point (a trysting place for lovers). My tutu kane told me this story and he really believes it. There were two young people who were very much in love but the family disapproved of their relationship and they were watched constantly, so they could never be alone. The young man

visited a kahuna Aloha who prom-
ised to help him in return for a
basket of eggs. The eggs were supplied and the kahuna turned the
young man into a shark so every
night he could swim from the
ocean through an underground
tunnel which led into the center
of the cave. His wahine met him
there every night unobserved. On
a very still night, if one is brave
enough to crawl through the narrow, dangerous inner cave, the
lovers' voices can be heard.

*A shark may
be a lover
in disguise.*

...the traditional villain of the sea is not *all* bad. At least not to the Hawaiians.

My mother-in-law lived with her grandparents as a child. Whenever her grandfather became ill, he instructed the young girl to go down to a particular spot on the shore and to feed the white shark that would be there. She obeyed and the shark was always there. When she returned home her grandfather had always recovered.

...some more on ti leaves...

My date and I were hiking at Sacred Falls. It was my first experience and as we crossed and re-crossed the mountain stream I was intrigued by seeing a ti leaf weighted down by a rock along the trail. Being anxious to be considered a kamaaina, I began to follow the custom and repeated the process all the way up to the falls.

Halfway up we were startled by a group of young people, pale and frightened, leaping down the trail as though they were being pursued by demons.

My date managed to stop one young hiker who breathlessly told him this story:

"Before this hike we were warned to be sure to follow the custom of leaving ti leaves on rocks as an offering to Kamapua'a, the Hog god. We didn't believe it so we refused to do it. While we were having lunch below the falls, where we had spread a cloth over a flat rock, we suddenly heard a loud "swish" from the air, and looked up just in time to see a huge boulder hurtling through space from the source of the falls. You won't believe this, but it landed exactly in the center of our lunch cloth. We just jumped up and ran. We will never come to this place again!"

...as for war souvenirs...

My old bed-ridden uncle objected violently when he heard I had hung a machete, obtained in the Philippines during the war, over the doorway of our home. He insisted it could result in great disaster and even death.

I laughed at his fears, calling him old-fashioned and superstitious, assuring him it was just a souvenir. Nothing happened until a week later. I woke up one morning and turned my head slightly on the pillow to find my face scraping against metal. The machete was imbedded in my pillow.

My old uncle lived on the opposite side of the Island and had not been out of his bed for three years! This same uncle thought nothing of the fact that over his own doorway the mummified body of a baby was displayed and revered as an aumakua of the family.

...a visitor almost lost his head showing off...

A tour group was being shown the sacrificial rock located at Kokekole Pass above· Schofield Barracks. One of the youths in the group laughed at the explanation the guide made and, jumping up, lay down on the rock and fitted his head in the groove provided for the victim's head, as had been done hundreds of years before. Everyone laughed nervously and the tour group moved on.

That night the young man found he could not move his head without extreme pain. When a kahuna was consulted, he said the boy was being punished for ridiculing a very sacred place. The boy recovered only after he made an appropriate offering to the gods of the heiau.

...a proper blessing must be performed...or spirits will hex a new building.

In the district of Moiliili there was an old Hawaiian church which stood for many years. Hundreds of Hawaiians were buried in the old graveyard behind the church. Burial places are very sacred to the Hawaiians as the bones of a person are felt to have mana. It was believed that an unscrupulous or evil person could do great harm if he obtained the bones.

In the interest of progress the church and surrounding grounds were sold and a modern high-rise apartment was built on the site, and a highway built over a section of the cemetery. The graves were first claimed by the families and removed as far as was possible.

The Hawaiian church members and many other sympathizers objected to the desecration, feeling that the proper rites had not been performed correctly.

Some years later a Fire Department captain and his men were ordered to make an inspection of the condominium. They arrived and had erected a ladder to its full extent. It was a still, cloudless day, one of those breathless, hot days when even a tiny wisp of a breeze would have been welcome. One of the firefighters had just crawled up to the third story of the building, when a powerful gust of wind of almost hurricane force whirled about the ladder with such intensity that he had to climb down to safety, clinging with whitened knuckles to the ladder steps until his feet touched the ground. No one spoke as the crew hastily packed up their equipment and literally raced back to their station. An unexplained wind is a warning that a spirit is present.

...Island builders know the value of a blessing...they have learned the hard way!

It is common knowledge that when the Wilson Tunnel was being built, several workmen were killed because the site was not properly blessed. As soon as the proper rites were performed the accidents ceased.

When the new Halawa Stadium was being constructed, there was no end of accidents, including the earth sinking, until the old Hawaiian blessing ceremony was carried out.

Not many people realize that our national Monument, Diamond Head, was once the site of a heiau and was considered sacred. A contractor was preparing to construct some buildings inside the crater and had all of his heavy earth-moving equipment moved in the night before. Arriving early in the morning for work, he saw every piece overturned on its side. The project was abandoned.

...one good turn deserves another...

An old lady who was very poor was well known to always share what little she had with others poorer than herself.

One early morning, she took her basket and went down to a certain section of the beach which was known for the opihi (shell fish) which clung to the rocks there. She squatted down on a huge flat rock projecting out over the water. The opihi were not abundant there but she was patient and had all the time in the world. As she laboriously pried at the rocks, she felt herself moving. Looking down, she discovered she was sitting on the back of a huge turtle. She did not dare move as he paddled slowly to another area where the opihi as well as limu kohu was abundant. When her basket was full he returned her to where she began.

A poor but unselfish old lady finds a surprise benefactor.

...so does one bad turn...

A young Hawaiian girl was on her way to church, wearing a new hat. Some naughty children made faces and threw dirt at her. The girl, in anger, spit in the face of the nearest child, a young boy.

During the night the girl became violently ill with a high fever. Her parents called for a ho'oponopono.

The girl's sister told about the incident of the day before and it was deduced that the insulted boy had told his parents, who in turn consulted the uhane (spirit), who reversed the spell and sent bad vibes back to the girl. She finally recovered after proper confession and restitution was made.

...the Nanakuli district was always arid and still is. However, Hawaiians have their own method of dealing with a water shortage...

A lost traveler going through that area many years ago kept inquiring of everyone he met, as to where he was and where he could find room and lodging. Every person he tried to talk to looked at him blankly and without a word continued on his way. Later, he reported to his friends how strange it was to find an entire village of people who were all deaf. He never found out that this was a well-thought-out plan on the part of the people. By feigning deafness, they gave out no information. The shortage of water was so acute they were unable and unwilling to share it with outsiders.

...and, then, there is the Hawaiian version of ESP...

An Hawaiian girl who was serving as a missionary in Africa was awakened from a deep sleep one night by the overwhelming fragrance of flowers. There were no flowers in her room or even growing anywhere near her house. She sat up in bed and turned on a light. To her horror, she glanced down on her arm and saw a "nahu akua," the marks of a spirit bite. It was in the shape of a human mouth with teeth marks.

She remembered the old Hawaiian belief that the "nahu akua" was a message from the spirit world telling her that a loved one was in danger of death. At first she panicked, knowing she was thousands of miles from home. Her Christian training told her to drop to her knees and pray for protection for the unknown one, which she did. The following day she received a cablegram informing her that her father had been accused of a serious crime and sentenced to death but at the last moment the real murderer had confessed and her father was acquitted.

...the next time you have a party, you may receive some unexpected guests...

In Waikiki, on Paokalani Avenue where surf-boards are stacked up on the beach today, there used to stand a home. Many years ago the residents were having a dinner party when everyone heard an eerie flapping sound. Rushing over to the stone wall facing the sea, they were horrified to see dozens of huge eels, writhing and slithering against the wall, their evil eyes glistening and their mouths agape. One of the party yelled at the other guests to bring any food they could lay their hands on. Everyone rushed to feed the hungry eels. As soon as they were satisfied they slithered away and were never seen again. The mystery was never solved, but aumakuas are known to dwell in eel form.

23

A "visitor" from the depths of the sea welcomes her long lost relative.

...there can be such a thing as too much family feeling...

Just before the last destructive tidal wave, my husband was returning from the North Shore where he had been surfing. The sun was beginning to set as he tucked his board under his arm and started toward the car. A touch on his shoulder forced him to turn his head toward the sea. No one else was on the beach at the time. About 100 feet from the shore, he saw a woman holding a baby. Her hair was streaming down her back and the water was up to her waist, although he knew the water at that particular spot was well over one's head.

The woman was smiling and beckoning to him. Instinctively, he started toward her but she kept backing away, although she continued to remain standing. All the old Hawaiian stories he had ever heard began to come to him and he turned and ran to his car and lost no time in returning home.

I talked to my grandmother about this and she told me that her own aunt and her child had been swept out to sea and drowned during a tidal wave many years before. Her explanation was that the aumakua (her dead aunt's spirit) was lonely and was trying to get him to follow her.

Heaven and Earth were personified as Wahea and Papa who gave birth to the gods.

The male gods of Hawaii are Kane, Lono, Kanaloa and Ku.

The major female gods were Mo'o or lizard goddesses such as Kihawahine, and Pele, the volcano goddess, still venerated today.

The gods who presided over crafts and professions were very important. Ku-alana-wao presided over canoe-making; Laka, the goddess of the hula, Ma'iola the practice of healing and medicine and Kapo, the god of the art of sorcery. Each man worshipped the akua that presided over his profession.

Kane was originally the only god of Hawaii. He first created night and then everything else.

Lono was the god of harvest and agriculture, also the god of medicine. His name is often mentioned in chants in regard to weather. Captain Cook was believed to be the god Lono in human form and was addressed as such.

Ku was the god of war and chiefs, god of the forest, canoe-making and fishing.

Kanaloa was the ocean god or the god of salt water. Many people believed that Kanaloa was not a god, just a servant of Kane, but others believed he was a true god because of the miracles he performed, especially in healing of the body. Hawaiian reckoning only went to 400,000, so the priests acknowledged allegiance to 400,000 gods. As such, there were more gods than people.

The Aumakuas were the family or personal gods and came in many forms, sometimes visible. They took the form of owls, lizards, rocks, plants, caterpillars, mice, fish or birds, even flames, thunder or lightning. The lizard was the most dreaded, the owl most beneficial, and the shark was a friend and protector. Idols made of ohia wood were purposely made ugly to inspire fear.

The Gods Of Hawaii

With the coming of the missionaries, efforts were made to tie in the three gods Kane, Ku, and Lono to the Biblical trinity and Kanaloa was considered the devil. The idea did not really "take."

The definition of "god" was complicated.

A great Lord above all things.

A spirit.

Power, strength, knowledge without death, without source.

A chief above all.

A corpse or a ghost.

A slave of the lower class.

A devil.

Three classes of gods were recognized:

Great gods.

Guardian spirits.

Things without souls.

There were many gods in the spirit class.

Spirits without bodies, aumakuas of Day or Light.

Aumakuas of night or darkness; these are the dead.

District chiefs. These were visible gods who had great power and were to be dreaded.

UNIHIPILI

This word, defined, means "the spirit of a dead person, sometimes believed to be present in the bones, blood, hair, or possessions of the deceased and kept reverently and with great love by the family."

A person who guarded and protected such remains was called a kahu. The bones or hair or whatever was left of the body after the flesh was disposed of, would be wrapped in tapa and sometimes kept in a calabash or other container in the home. It was deified, offered food and called upon for guidance but was not considered an aumakua.

A great deal of responsibility rested on the kahu because he could use the unihipili for good or evil purposes. This is seldom heard of today.

If a family or individual wished to be free of his unihipili, this could be done with a special ritual of "letting go" and the deceased's remains would be released to enter Po and become one of the aumakua.

KUPUA

The kupua were demi-gods who were different from other gods because they lacked the power of the akua and had none of the loving nature or close earthly ties of the aumakua.

They remained in specific localities and were capable of taking on various forms. Most often the form was a rock or a stone. They also could be male or female. They were peaceful deities unless they were mistreated. However, they disliked being moved — as some visitors have discovered to their misfortune. In modern times, people who are "rock-hounds" or just happen to pick up an unusual rock as a souvenir and who take it home with them, claim they have had bad luck or accidents befall them. The same is true of pieces of lava taken from the volcano area. The management of the Volcano House on the Island of Hawaii receives packages containing pieces of lava or rock from all over the world from visitors who have carried them away and are now anxious to right the wrong.

PELE

The goddess Pele is the best-known and most revered of all gods and goddesses, and is still worshipped in modern times.

She has several forms. Those who have "encountered" her describe her as a beautiful, young woman with flowing hair which can be black, blonde, or, if she is angry, red. The latter colors are unlike the natural coloring of the Hawaiian people, but since they are contained in the range of volcano colors, it is not difficult to understand the Hawaiians' description of the goddess.

She was just as often seen as an old hag. Whether young or old, she was often accompanied by a small dog.

Hundreds of stories are recounted by Hawaiians and non-Hawaiians about driving down a road and seeing either the young woman or the old hag walking or just standing by the side of the road. It was considered bad luck not to offer her a ride. She would never speak, and before the car or wagon would reach its destination she would disappear. If she was not offered a ride, the car would mysteriously stall somewhere along the way.

Pele had a dual nature, both peaceful and benign, as well as fiery, angry and unpredictable. While she is capable of doing great acts of kindness for her people, with little or no warning, she can be extremely destructive. When angry, she would stamp her foot, causing earthquakes followed by eruptions of molten lava and fire, as she vented her uncontrollable temper if she was denied something she wanted or was made jealous. Thus did the Hawaiians explain the capriciousness of Mother Nature.

Pele's full name was Pele-honua-mea (Pele, the sacred earth person).

She came to the Island of Hawaii by way of Maui where she had formed the great crater of Hale-a-ka-la (House of the Sun).

THE HEIAUS

A heiau was an ancient Hawaiian place of worship, generally a stone platform or a simple terraced piece of land. There are many of them preserved today in Hawaii. Some of the heiaus still remaining today are Keaiwa on

If a law breaker (kapu breaker) could not be found, a slave was chosen for sacrifice. He was so despised that he was required to wear a particular tattoo on his forehead. It consisted of a dot, a crescent and a pyramid. This tattoo, or at least the dot on the forehead,

Religion and Kapus

Aiea Heights, Puu o Mahuka at Waimea and Ulupo near the Kailua Road.

The Hawaii rulers had two orders of priests, the priests of Ku and the priests of Lono. The Ku rituals were held in connection with war and the Lono rituals were for maintaining peace and the agriculture of the land.

The Ku ceremonies were held in heiaus called luakini, and in them alone, human sacrifices could be held.

The Mu was the name given the public executioner. His job was to procure victims for human sacrifice and to execute kapu breakers. Children were threatened by telling them, "If you aren't good the Mu will get you!" The Mu clubbed his victim senseless before offering him up for sacrifice.

Women were seldom, if ever, used as a sacrifice; only prisoners-of-war, kapu breakers or slaves.

The slaves were called "kauwa" and were the most despised of all creatures. Untouchable and outcast, they lived apart from everyone else and were drawn on for sacrificial victims.

This class was often linked with the menehunes.

could never be erased, so slaves had to hide out until 1819 when the kapu system was abolished.

They were described as "filthy beasts." If they bore children out of their class, the children's necks were wrung like chickens. A slave must also keep his head covered with tapa when in the presence of other classes. If he wished to be released from this curse, he was allowed to drown himself; someone would hold his head under the water and chant, "Lie still in the sea of the Lord."

The only place a kauwa was allowed to go was to the place of the chief who was his lord. His head was always covered and his eyes must remain downcast.

When a kauwa was needed for a sacrifice, he could not refuse to go. If he was not to be killed immediately, he was put on a "waiting list" by means of a gourd hanging from his neck.

The highest insult a person could give another was to say his ancestor had worn such a gourd, or in other words, he was a "nothing" person.

27

THE KAPU SYSTEM

The word, "Kapu" is the same as taboo, meaning prohibited, forbidden, sacred, holy, consecrated. Today you will find signs posted all over the Islands saying "Kapu", which also means "keep out."

Under the early rulers of Hawaii (kings, chiefs, priests), there existed the kapu system, consisting of so many "do's" and "do nots" that it was impossible for everyone to remember and observe them all. Dire punishment and death followed swiftly when a kapu was broken.

Women especially were considered "second class citizens" and the kapus they were forced to remember and practice were myriad.

In the matter of eating, in particular, there were many foods which were prohibited to women. For example:

Pork was prohibited because it was a feast food for gods, chiefs and priests. It was also related to Lono as Kamapuaa, the Hog God.

Bananas, because the banana tree was considered a body of the god, Kanaloa.

Coconuts, because the coconut tree was the body of Ku, also called the Erect.

Ulua fish. This was offered to the god Ku in his war ritual in place of a human sacrifice.

The fish Kumu (a red goat fish). This was used in a ceremony when the main post of a new sleeping house was dedicated.

Niuhi (the Great White Shark). This was the symbol of the High Chief.

Palaoa (whale), a form of the god Kanaloa. The whale's tooth was a symbol reserved for the Alii.

Honu (sea turtle).

'Ea (sea tortoise).

Nuao (porpoise).

Hahalua (spotted sting ray).

All of these were considered a form of the god Kanaloa.

Men and women cooked their food separately and certain men's houses were kapu to women. Women also had a separate house for childbirth.

Canoe-building, the making of nets and hooks, fishing and tending the fields, were carried out by men only. Any implement or equipment used by a man was kapu to women. The touch of a female would ruin it.

Kapu breaker punished.

The population was strictly divided into two classes, the aristocrats and the commoners. This division depended on the power of kapu, which was a magic word.

Mana was a spiritual power and everything — human, animal, or inanimate objects — contained it. All men had good mana, all women had bad.

The exchange of clothing, especially anything worn next to the skin, was kapu.

It was kapu to use a sleeping mat for anything except sleeping upon. A head pillow was not to be sat on or to put one's feet on.

In the matter of eating poi, the dipping of two fingers into the bowl and transferring it to the mouth was correct; to use three fingers was greedy, and to use just one was a sign of stinginess.

In Hawaiian worship, it was considered kapu to labor, fish or plant during certain days of the month which were set aside for worship in the temples of the different gods. For example, the days and nights of the first two nights of the new moon were sacred to Ku. The days preceding the full moon belonged to Lono. The twenty-third and twenty-fourth were sacred to Kanaloa and the twenty-seventh and twenty-eighth were sacred to Kane.

During the Makahiki, the season in honor of the God, Lono, all sorts of kapus were laid upon the people. It was a time of harvest and bounty for those in high places. Lesser chiefs who served as governors collected the offering-tax such as animals, feathers, cloth, and tools. All of these were given to persons of high rank, which included the king, his nobles, and prominent priests of the land.

Spiritual power, as represented by mana, could be obtained by obeying the king. The king, alone, brought mana directly from the gods. No man could touch the king, his garment or his shadow. To break this kapu meant death.

When a canoe was made, pigs and dogs were sacrificed so that mana could enter it. On some important occasions when a human sacrifice was required, word would get around. Those who felt they might be eligible fled into the forests and mountain tops.

Men with mana had to protect themselves from defilement by women. Men were of the light and women of the darkness, men were strong and women weak, men were clean, women impure. Women must not eat with men or watch men eat or touch food meant for men. Kapu foods to women were pigs, coconuts, certain fish, and, of course, the banana. For a woman to eat a banana was to risk death by instant strangulation if she were found out, since the banana was created by the gods to represent men's fertility.

On days of menstruation, women were locked up in a tiny room. To protest or try to escape could mean death for the woman or anyone helping her.

The commoners lived in constant fear of breaking the kapus. They not only had to work hard as farmers and fishermen, but were always subject to the whims of their superiors.

Fishing, a main livelihood of the land, had its share of kapus to plague the islanders.

On the day when a fisherman was going out to sea, no one in his family was allowed to ask where he was going.

While he was away, his wife must not gossip, or visit or entertain anyone until his return.

No bananas must be carried with him on his way to sea. Bananas were unlucky to the fisherman.

Contact with any of the Alii class was also very dangerous to the commoner. A commoner's shadow must not fall on a king; also, no commoner should ever be on a level higher than the King. To come into the presence of the King with a wet head could mean death. A commoner must prostrate himself not only in the presence of the Alii, but he must also do the same if he sees food or water carried into the King's house.

A sailor on a vessel of any kind must not allow himself to be on a deck higher than where the King was standing.

The story is told of two young princesses who were caught bathing in the King's private swimming pool. Their tutor was immediately killed for failing to teach them any better.

If the shadow of a man fell upon the house of a kapu chief or if it fell on the back of the chief or upon his malo or anything he owned, death was the punishment.

Anyone who passed through the doorway of a kapu chief or climbed over his stockade or even stepped unknowingly on the chief's footprint hidden in the grass, could also be put to death.

Stoning, strangulation, clubbing and burning until the body was reduced to ashes, were the methods used to put men to death.

In the year 1819, Liholiho, the son and successor of Kamehameha the Great, abolished the kapus of the ancient religion. In a dramatic gesture of defiance, he sat and ate in public with his mother. This was a turning point in history. With the destruction of the old kapu system, the old religion died also. The Hawaiians were ripe for Christianity.

Many opposed the abolition of the old religion. They rallied under the leadership of Kekuaokalani, a priest under Kamehameha. He gathered an army to prepare to fight the destroyers of the gods and temples. Their war cry was "Ka-aua-kapu!" (Hold fast to the kapus!)

This battle was fought on the plains of South Kona and Kekuaokalani was killed and his followers dispersed.

King Liholiho, son and successor to Kamehameha the Great, abolished the ancient kapus of Hawaii.

Dream Lore

Dreams and their meanings were very important to the early Hawaiians and still are, even in modern times, although they are not discussed as freely today.

The Hawaiian world was filled with spirits, both good and evil. The good spirits were generally the aumakuas (ancestral gods), the spirits of the dead who were always present to warn, chastise, guide, and advise.

One of the ways the aumakua contacted the living was through dreams. Interpreting a dream was serious business, and more often than not, a qualified kahuna or an elder was called on for the true interpretation. After the Islands were Christianized, searching the Bible for guidance was added to the old ways. In fact, even today, both methods are employed.

It is believed by some that everyone is possessed of two spirits, one that operates while a person is awake and the other when he is asleep, taking turns, as it were.

It is dangerous to awaken a sleeping person before he wakes up naturally himself, as perhaps that wandering spirit has not had time to return from his errands which are what we call dreams.

The entry and exit spot for dreams is called "lua'uhane", the spirit hole, which is located in the outer corner of the eye or a tear duct.

Some of the interpretations of dreams are similar to those of other cultures, while others are uniquely Polynesian and, even among the experts in the field, many meanings are contradictory.

Bananas, which are bad luck for a fisherman, are also a symbol of wealth or gain, as is the coconut or, more specifically, a bunch of coconuts.

To dream of a lizard is a good omen for an Hawaiian as it could signify the presence of one's aumakua.

If one dreams of the hair falling out or of having a haircut, this is a sign of loss of virility.

If a woman dreams of losing an eyelid, she has, or will lose, her virginity.

A dream of being buried alive stands for the birth experience.

A tooth being pulled: a death in the family.

Birds flying in the house is a sign of death, yet in some cultures this is a happy omen.

If one dreams of a bowl of poi fermenting and overflowing, a thief will be exposed.

Descent into a cave with no way out indicates lunacy.

Someone wearing black or lilac indicates a sign of death.

Observing the right side of the body means one is looking at the moral side, but the left side indicates immorality or inferiority.

Seeing one's own shadow is to see one's worst side.

If a person dreams he is crawling, he shows signs of the desire to return to childhood.

To dream of fish eyes, especially disembodied ones, shows one's desire for perpetual attention.

If the number five (5) is emphasized in a dream, this means good luck as five is a "nature number" because the body is made up of fives (the fingers and toes); also, the head, arms and legs total five.

A crater or hole signifies death to the Hawaiians. In other cultures it means the womb.

To dream of volcanoes means repressed passions or impulses erupting to the surface.

Dreams of salt water indicate death but sweet water means restored health.

To dream of a koa tree means riches.

To see a canoe in a dream is a bad omen.

To change clothes with someone normally means bad luck to an Hawaiian. If it happens in a dream, it means that the dreamer is trying to change his ways or his nature.

Dreams of ashes indicate humiliation and belittlement.

Vermin in the house mean an unwanted pregnancy.

If a man dreams of a burning house, he will quarrel with his wife.

Flying a kite in a cemetery — life in the midst of death.

A dream of cannibalism means one is taking possession of another's ideas or mana.

Seeing a new moon means magic; a full moon, madness.

All journeys in a dream foretell death; the same applies when dreaming of seeing a sleeping person.

An encounter with a squid or octopus means a possessive and clinging mother.

If one dreams, he himself is dead, he is afraid of life and desires to retreat from it.

Dreaming of carrying a great weight on the back and shoulders and being unable to be rid of it, indicates a resentment because of too much responsibility.

To dream of an earthquake means one's life will be disrupted.

To the Hawaiian, the butterfly is a symbol of freedom and happiness; in other cultures it represents the departed soul which has taken flight.

To dream of a baby being passed from one person's hands to another, shows the desire to be rid of responsibility.

A dream of mangos foretells a prosperous year ahead.

Dreams, to be interpreted correctly, depend on a combination of circumstances and other conditions and happenings, so only a qualified kahuna (an expert in his field) can correctly interpret a dream.

The writer was present during the following incident, which I am told is quite unique.

Two young Hawaiian boys had been hunting wild boar in the Ka'u district on the Island of Hawaii. They killed one and brought it home to the family ranch in their jeep. Although exhausted, they found it difficult to sleep that night, especially the younger boy.

Those of us who were sleeping in an adjoining room were suddenly awakened about midnight by an unearthly scream coming out of the boys' room. We rushed in and found the younger boy racing around the room, screaming, looking down at his hands and trying to wipe them clean on his shorts. He later said he thought they were covered with the boar's blood.

Without warning, he leaped on the bed of the older boy who was still asleep and clutched him tightly, begging him to help him escape from the open mouth and fangs of the boar who was hovering over them. The other boy began to scream also and the two of them with arms entwined leaped off the bed and huddled in an opposite corner of the room. Their eyes were open but glazed with fright and they both were trembling and soaked with perspiration.

We awakened them gently and when they were able to talk, they both gave the same story (dream) that the disembodied head of the boar was floating over their beds accusing them of its murder. Needless to say, they took no part the next day in the luau in which the boar was the featured entree.

We are told it is possible for two people to share a dream simultaneously but it is a very rare and unusual experience.

Dream-mating was not uncommon among the early Hawaiians.

Women claimed to have a kane o ka po, or a man would have a wahine o ka po, spirit lover. These lovers only visited them at night and they had great adventures together. If an unusual child was born to a woman with perhaps some animal characteristics, or if a fetus miscarried, resembled a fish or rock, it was explained as a "spirit baby."

One such child grew to maturity and developed a strange skin condition, with white patches over most of his skin (actually just a pigment deficiency), but he was respected and almost worshipped because it was believed his father must have been an aumakua in lizard form.

Portents

When one hears the word "portent," the first picture that comes to mind is of a black-clothed person standing over a huge caldron, stirring up mysterious potions, while muttering evil incantations and prophesying evil happenings.

Actually, the word means a sign, an omen, forewarnings, threatenings of forebodings and was a very important and useful part of life among the Hawaiian people.

The people were, and still are, very close to nature as well as life after death. We see this especially in their beliefs regarding the aumakua, the souls who have died and entered the spirit world. Although dead, they are still considered members of the 'ohana (family), communicating with the living by advising, warning, and instructing.

Portents were present in many things, particularly nature. Wind, rainbows, clouds, strange behaviour of animals or the flight pattern of birds.

Portents are also present very vividly in dreams, visions, and supernatural voices. Sometimes a chilling of the skin, a prickling of the scalp, an unusual scent, or just an unexplainable premonition is considered a portent and often needs interpretation by an expert.

An interesting and chilling ritual that could be carried out to bring to light a crime or an evil deed was called the "kuni" ritual. Kuni means to burn.

If a person became critically ill or died and it was suspected that it had occurred because of sorcery, it was possible to reverse the spell. Hair, nails, or clothing of the victim would be burned and the ashes scattered in the path of the suspected sorcerer. Accompanied by the proper incantations, the sorcerer would be killed. Sometimes the face of the enemy could be seen in the flames, exposing him and his evil deed.

By this ritual, a portent could be avoided or resolved. In post-Christianity days, the Bible was also used for explanation and guidance.

There was a star called Kane which was only visible to priests and astrologers. It sometimes appeared above the moon. It was known to be a portent of the death of a king. When it appeared, the king was carefully guarded and stayed close to home.

Disasters were often avoided by studying the position of the stars. Travelers were also guided this way, avoiding dangerous days.

Portents were seen in the eyes of the dead. If at death the eyes were closed and then opened several hours later, it was a sign the corpse was looking for someone. If a relative died shortly afterward, it was said it was because the corpse had opened its eyes and was looking for him. If tears flowed from the eyes of the dead, it was a sign of great affection for the living. If the corpse suddenly became very heavy while it was being carried, it was believed the departed one did not want to go.

It is a scientific fact today that animals have an unusual and acute awareness of impending natural disasters. The Hawaiians have known this for centuries. Just before an earthquake, a volcanic eruption, or tidal wave, many animals become extremely agitated, running around in an erratic manner and fleeing in fright. Many times, their eyes become dilated and often the hair on the back bristled and would stand up straight. Dogs howled when a death was imminent and owls had a certain cry for the same reason.

Clouds and cloud formations had many meanings.

One who was an expert in this field was called "kilokilo," an astronomer priest. He was very important to the king who depended on him for advice on how to conduct the affairs of state.

Wrapping himself in tapa, he spent many hours scanning the skies and clouds for portents. He understood the meaning according to the shape, color, and movement.

If clouds were long and narrow, like a cluster of leaves with the leaves hanging down, rain and wind would follow. If they pointed up, the weather would be calm. If a cloud lay smoothly over the mountain in the morning, it foretold rain. If the sky was overcast with no wind, the forecast was a real thunder and lightning storm.

If a rainbow was seen with the rain, it would be a short rain, if accompanied by wind, a long rain. Big drops meant a short rain, and small fine drops meant an extended rain.

The color of the sky was significant also, a blue black sky at sunset predicted high surf.

A small ring around the moon foretold the arrival of large schools of fish. A large ring, a storm.

Unusually rough and high waves and crashing surf meant the death of a great chief.

Also, the spirit of a departed person could take on the form of a cloud.

There are many omens which take various forms in the old Hawaiian beliefs. Some of them are familiar to other cultures, such as an itchy palm portends money one is to receive; or, a sudden unexplained wind causing a chill, portends evil. These, among others, seem to be universal.

Hawaiians are so akin to nature that many of these portents are related to the wind, rocks, rain, rainbows, etc.

Dreams, visions, skin sensations, clouds, the *nahu akua* (spirit bite), voices or unusual odors, pleasant and otherwise, all of these were very real and meaningful to the old timers and have been carried over to the present.

Bones And Caves

What's so special about bones?
To the ancient Hawaiians they were sacred; the last, clean portion of the once alive person.

When a man died, his flesh became corrupt, even his blood, but his immortality lay in his bones. They were guarded carefully, respected, loved or deified by the family and used for evil purposes by the enemy.

In pre-Christian days, it was the custom to remove the flesh (pela) from the bones and sink it into the sea. Only members of the family could do this. In the event of the death of royalty, it was done by trusted, blood-related retainers. A purifying ritual was required after handling a deceased person.

Deification of bones was done by a ritual called, "unihipili"; this kept the spirit in the bones. The bones retained the personality of the person.

When someone was reluctant to let the deceased "go," he could keep that loved one near by keeping the bones. In ancient days, a common sight was a calabash hanging from the rafters of an Hawaiian home, containing the skull of a dead relative. It was not uncommon for a person to clean the leg and arm bones and skull of a lover, husband or wife, wrap it carefully in clean material and take it to bed with them. It was felt this kept the spirit alive.

The unihipili spirit could be called on to aid the owner or keeper.

Desecration of the bones meant desecration of the spirit, so secret burial places were sought. A person's enemies could do great evil if they could acquire his bones. The bones and grave of Kamehameha the Great have never been located, so well hidden have they been.

Many rumors exist, trying to pinpoint possible locations. The cliffs above Kaaawa on the North Shore of Oahu are one of many places reportedly full of hidden caves filled with royal bones and great treasure, but to date, no one has found either cave or treasure. The hiding cave is called Pohukaina. Either the burial caves are too well concealed or probably blocked up or, because of the terrain, they are inaccessible. Or, perhaps, they are simply not located there at all.

Iao is the famous burial cave of Maui. The last great chief to be buried there was in 1736, but there is no one living today who knows the entrance.

Waiuli, on Maui, is the site of a deep pit where the bones of the common people were thrown.

There is also a disposal pit called Kaaawa inside the crater of Haleakala, on Maui.

In the burial cave of Pu'uwepa in Kohala, Hawaii, are the bones of Pa'ao, the famous kahuna who built the heiau of Mo'okini at Kohala. Its entrance is said to be beneath the sea.

Another burial pit is located in the pali of Molilele, in Ka'u, Hawaii.

Desecration of bones can be done several ways. Exposing them to the sunlight was an insult. Using the skull as a spittoon, or, complete destruction of the bones, was a desecration; for then, the spirit could never join its aumakua. Making fish hooks from bones was insulting, although the leg bones of a white man were considered useful and were greatly sought after by some unprincipled people who believed they brought good fishing luck.

Burning of bones was only done to the enemy.

Today, many Hawaiians cling to the old ways, abhorring cremation. However, scattering the ashes of a loved one at sea, or a burial at sea, is accepted by some.

If a family was of the lineage of Pele, bodies were hidden away until the flesh had decomposed, then the carefully cleaned bones were taken to the Kilauea firepit where, accompanied by the proper gifts, prayers and offerings, they were thrown into the pit. In this way the uhane (spirit) lived forever with Pele, the fire goddess. If the deceased one was not acceptable to Pele, the body was thrown back to the officiating priest and was then returned to a burial cave.

It was also customary to bury the bundle of bones under the dwelling house.

Bones were sometimes kept in a specially constructed little grave-house which often was located near the family home, or was built over the grave. It contained belongings of the departed one: clothes and jewelry, and keepsakes. Fresh food was constantly supplied for the use of the spirit.

There is a well-known little grave-house in Ka'u, Hawaii, complete with curtains, a completely made bed, a dresser filled with the clothing and personal articles of the deceased, and a table complete with dishes on which food is placed daily.

To prevent the bones of a person, particularly one of the ali'i rank, from being discovered and desecrated, funeral processions were often carried out at night, in secrecy, with no wailing at the time. Sometimes, the corpse would be carried to its burial place by a devious route.

Caves containing skeletons have been discovered as late as 1966 on the Kona Coast, a favorite sight-seeing tour for visitors from nearby hotels. But, from objects found alongside the bodies, it is believed they were fairly recent burials. The objects were pipes and kerosene lanterns, burlap, etc. Such things were not known or used by the ancient Hawaiians.

On an expedition in 1966, forty cave burial sites were discovered on the desolate Kona Coast. Fortunately, there are laws preventing people from disturbing burial sites, so they were left intact.

The Hawaiians of old were clever and devious in hiding the bones of their loved ones, and especially the beloved ali'i. At great danger to their own lives, they carried corpses up and over dangerous cliffs, through treacherous underground lava tubes and subterranean caves, blocking up and closing off entrances and exits so that their dead would be protected throughout eternity from desecration.

Are the spirits who still live in those hidden bones aware of who they are and where they are and of the tremendous danger and sacrifice their keepers went through to protect them?

Kamehameha the Great united the Hawaiian Islands and ruled with a stern but just hand. At his death, his bones were hidden in a secret cave. To this day, the burial place remains a mystery.

Hawaiian legend said that Lono, who was the god of rain and fertility, harvest, and prosperity, had quarreled with his wife, and left home. He wandered aimlessly, engaging in boxing matches with anyone he met. Finally, he sailed away, promising to return at some future date.

When Captain Cook made his appearance, the priests of Lono proclaimed him as the long absent god. They honored him with every honor fit

Captain Cook was struck from behind, stabbed, and clubbed to death.

A chief informed Midshipman Vancouver that Cook's body had been carried ashore but that King Kalaniopuu assured them it would be returned. The Hawaiians were warned that if Cook's body was not returned by morning, the whole village would be destroyed. It was later discovered that the Hawaiians had taken cover in a remote cave on a cliff after Cook's death.

What *REALLY* Happened To Captain Cook's Body?

for the god. He was draped with fine feathered capes, fed the finest food, and became the close friend of King Kalaniopuu, the ruling ali'i. Whenever the Captain stepped ashore, the beaches emptied miraculously. Commoners kept out of sight according to the law of kapu.

Good feeling between Cook and the Hawaiians continued, but much of it was on the surface. Underneath the trade and friendly exchanges were the usual instances of petty thievery and deceit. Cook's officers trusted neither the Hawaiian ali'i nor their priests of Lono, especially the wily Koa. Whatever the Hawaiians thought of "Lono" and his men, they continued to steal; they not only stole nails ("even the sheathing nails out of the ship's bottom") but they also stole knives and other such articles. Many of these articles were traced back to the ali'i themselves.

On February 4, Cook sailed from Kealakekua, Hawaii, in search of a better harbor. However, due to bad weather, the *Resolution* damaged her foremast and he was back in a week's time. They would have to remain in Kealakekua for the time it took to repair the ship.

Several incidents of further thievery followed and trouble kept mounting until, finally, in a fight on the beach between the natives and white men,

That same night, one of the priests and another man, under the cover of darkness approached the ship with a horrendous bundle. It contained only parts of Cook's body, "mostly from his hind parts," which was all they were able to get, but they said that Kalaniopuu and other chiefs still had the head and bones.

Finally, Kalaniopuu told the chiefs they must give back Captain Cook's bones. A meeting was arranged on the beach with the flying of white flags and the beating of drums. A chief handed over the remains of the Captain, wrapped in tapa cloth and covered with a cloak of black and white feathers. The bundle contained the Captain's hands (recognized because of a well-known scar), the scalp, and the skull. Only the hands had some flesh on them in which holes had been made and filled with salt. The other parts of the body which had escaped the fire had been distributed among the chiefs.

A naval burial service was read after the chiefs tried to make amends by putting a kapu on the beach. Then, Captain Cook's bones were lowered into the sea.

In years to come, the missionaries criticized Cook for blasphemy, in allowing the Hawaiians to venerate him as a god.

Epilogue

As burdensome and oppressive as the old kapus were, Hawaiians were to find that after the Christianization of the Islands and the coming of the missionaries, they had to contend with a different set of kapus.

However, they did have a short period when there were *no* kapus and *no* religion.

In 1819, they had repudiated their old gods, and it would not be until 1820 that the missionaries would arrive and begin their teachings.

Among many people, today, there is the belief that the missionaries forced their religious teaching upon the Hawaiian people. In fact, the missionaries arrived at the request of a young Hawaiian named Henry Opukahaia (or "Obookiah" as he was called by New Englanders) who had been converted while visiting New England.

Concerned with his people's moral and spiritual plight, he begged the mission board to send help to his people, which they did. As a result, they arrived when the "fields were ripe unto the harvest."

Royalty, as well as thousands of commoners, accepted Christianity and outwardly there were startling changes.

One of the most notable triumphs for the missionary cause happened in December 1824 when the high chiefess,

Kapiolani, an early convert to Christianity, decided to publicly defy the goddess, Pele. Pele, the goddess of the volcano, was still worshipped by many Hawaiians, even after their other gods had been abolished.

Accompanied by about fifty terrified followers, she descended into the crater, after eating the sacred ohelo berries which had formerly been kapu. Fearlessly, she shouted:

Jeohvah is my God. He kindled these fires. If I perish by the anger of Pele, then you may fear the power of Pele, but if I trust in Jehovah and He shall save me from the wrath of Pele when I break through her kapus, then you must fear and serve Jehovah God!

She emerged unharmed from the crater and many converts were made that day.

Her heroism spread around the world and fifty years later, Alfred Lord Tennyson, poet laureate of England, wrote a poem telling of Kapiolani's bravery.

However, in the hearts and minds of many Hawaiians, there continued to be agonizing conflict. They were torn between Christianity and the old religion. Beliefs in and the fear of the old powerful gods were deeply ingrained. To this day, some Hawaiians continue to experience this division of faith.

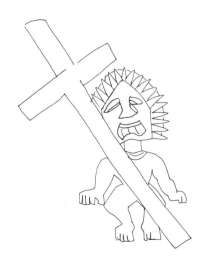